MUFFINS and QUICK BREADS

with Schmecks Appeal

MUFFINS and QUICK BREADS
with Schmecks Appeal

EDNA STAEBLER

McGraw-Hill Ryerson
Montreal   Toronto

McClelland & Stewart
Toronto

First published in 1990 by

McGraw-Hill Ryerson Limited
330 Progress Avenue
Scarborough, Canada
M1P 2Z5

McClelland & Stewart Limited
481 University Avenue
Toronto, Canada
M5G 2E9

ISBN 0-7710-8284-3

1 2 3 4 5 6 7 8 9 0   W   9 8 7 6 5 4 3 2 1 0

Canadian Cataloguing in Publication Data

Staebler, Edna   - date.
  Muffins and quick breads with schmecks appeal

(Schmecks appeal cookbook series)
ISBN 0-7710-8284-3

1. Muffins. 2. Bread. 3. Cookery, Mennonite.
4. Cookery - Ontario - Waterloo (Regional
municipality). I. Title. II. Series: Staebler,
Edna,   - date. Schmecks appeal cookbook series.

TX769.S73 1990   641.8′15   C90-094259-2

∞ This book was manufactured using acid-free paper.

Printed and bound in Canada

CONTENTS

INTRODUCTION

*Muffins and quick breads are members of the same family.
In both the dry ingredients are blended with the liquids
only enough to moisten the flour. Many quick bread recipes
make glorious muffins, and some of the muffin batter might
make a good quick bread.*

*Muffins are baked in 20 minutes; quick breads take
almost an hour. Both freeze very well; fruity quick breads
improve with age and will keep moist for a week — if
allowed to.*

MUFFINS

I was making muffins years before there were muffin shops on street corners, in shopping malls and in Toronto's Union Station. Mine are not monster muffins like those you can buy for a dollar apiece; baked in medium muffin tins, mine are a size that you can comfortably enjoy eating three or four of at a sitting.

My dear neighbour, Belle (she died this year, age 89), used to say to me, "You and your muffins!" because in the 32 years I've lived beside her cottage I've probably baked thousands. I constantly make muffins because I love to eat them and because they are the fastest thing I can think of to make when I know someone will soon be coming for a cup of tea.

If any muffins are left over, they can be placed on a cookie sheet in the freezer until they are frozen, then stored in plastic bags. Quickly heated, they are a godsend in an emergency, and when reheated taste as good as when they first came out of the oven.

Muffins can rise to almost any occasion: savoury ones are perfect with soup or a salad or to supplement a meal; bran muffins can make a complete healthy breakfast; nothing is better with a cup of afternoon tea; they'll even do in a pinch as a dessert.

Basic Muffins

*Muffins can't miss. Overbeating is their only hazard. The
batter should look lumpy and drop from the spoon in a
blob. If you use an electric mixer or blender for anything
but blending the liquid ingredients, or if you stir until the
batter is smooth and elastic (forming long strands when
the spoon is lifted), your muffins have had it. You can bake
them, of course, but they'll probably have tunnels and
holes, or be tough, dry, and insipid. If you blend the
ingredients just enough to barely moisten the flour, your
muffins will have a smooth, moist, even texture and a puffy
top, and be golden and glossy. If you serve them hot, you
don't have to split and butter them — unless you crave
extra bother and calories.*

BASIC MUFFIN RECIPE

This is just a starter; make your muffins taste better by adding
whatever appeals to you — grated cheese, bacon bits, spices,
cranberries, nuts, raisins, currants, dates, fresh fruit, coconut.

Fresh fruits greatly enhance the basic muffin but they don't
freeze well or even keep more than a day. But how could they?
You're sure to eat every one of them before the day is over.

Better stick to some proven recipes until you've got the hang
of it and become an addict, like me.

> **2 cups flour**
> **2 tablespoons sugar**
> **2½ teaspoons baking powder**
> **½ teaspoon salt**
> **1 egg, well beaten**
> **1 cup milk**
> **¼ cup melted butter or oil**

Sift together the flour, sugar, baking powder, and salt. Blend
the egg, milk, and butter. Add the liquid mixture to the dry; stir
only until the flour is moistened. Do not beat. Spoon into 12
well-greased muffin cups; fill each about two-thirds full. Bake
20 to 25 minutes at 400°F and serve immediately.

SUBSTITUTIONS

When you substitute an ingredient you like for one you don't like, or don't have, don't be too daring: use something not unlike what the recipe calls for in texture or density or flavour. Also remember that twice as much isn't necessarily twice as good.

I have had thousands of friendly letters from people who use *Food That Really Schmecks, More Food That Really Schmecks,* and *Schmecks Appeal.* Most of them tell me they've never had a failure when using the recipes. I think that is wonderful — and amazing. I can't say the same myself; it must mean that the recipes are good and reliable, that they really work if you follow them.

It's my own fault if I have occasional failures because I seldom follow a recipe exactly. I like trying different things to see what will happen. In that way I've come up with new recipes that are pretty special: like Ginger Raisin Muffins (page 40), Orange and Grapefruit Peel Muffins (page 23), tough-crusted little Breakfast Bran Muffins (page 30), and others.

WARM MUFFINS

Never serve a cold muffin. If there are any left over, they can be frozen for the next emergency. To reheat them, wrap loosely in foil and put them in a hot oven for 5 minutes, or use a bun warmer, or a heavy covered pot on top of the stove, turned low, or a toaster oven or microwave. Most of your friends will eat three or four, which doesn't leave many for next time, does it?

If you have to buy muffin tins, be sure to get seamless ones.

TOPPINGS FOR MUFFINS AND QUICK BREADS

If you want to give your muffins and quick breads an extra touch, sprinkle them with whatever you think is appropriate: sugar, sugar blended with cinnamon, chopped nuts, or seeds, bits or pieces of fruit, a crumble topping, grated cheese, maple butter, an icing sugar glaze, granola, jam, marmalade, bacon bits, grated lemon or orange rind blended with sugar, coconut, chocolate chips. Especially wonderful with some muffins is a sugar cube dipped briefly in a liqueur or whisky or rum and placed on top before baking.

MRS. CLEASON SCHMIDT'S BOILED RAISIN MUFFINS

The flavour is enhanced by boiling the raisins before you put them into the batter.

¾ to 1 cup raisins
1½ cups boiling water
½ cup shortening
¾ cup brown sugar
1 egg, well beaten
½ teaspoon salt
1 teaspoon vanilla
1½ cups flour
1 teaspoon baking powder
1 teaspoon baking soda

Simmer the raisins and water in a covered pot for about 20 minutes, then let them cool. Cream the shortening and sugar together, beat in the egg, salt, and vanilla till creamy. Add the cooled raisins and water. Sift the flour, baking powder, and baking soda into the mixture and stir only until moistened. Spoon into buttered muffin pans, about 1½ dozen. Bake at 350°F for 20 to 25 minutes.

GRAPENUTS MUFFINS

A hard crispy crust and mysterious little crunchy bits in a soft moist inside make these disappear far too quickly — but you can make more in 25 minutes. Keep the oven hot.

2 cups grapenuts
1¼ cups flour
½ cup sugar
2 teaspoons baking powder
1 teaspoon salt
⅓ cup oil
1 cup milk
1 teaspoon vanilla

Mix all the dry ingredients. Blend the oil, milk, and vanilla; pour the mixture over the dry ingredients and stir just enough to moisten. Spoon into well-buttered muffin tins, sprinkling more grapenuts on top. Bake in a 400°F oven for about 20 minutes. Cool on a rack. Serve warm. They'll be chewy and won't need any butter.

GRANOLA MUFFINS

Made in exactly the same way as grapenuts muffins but with **granola** instead of grapenuts, ⅓ **cup molasses** and ¼ **cup brown sugar** instead of ½ cup white sugar. You might need a little less milk or a little more flour. Great flavour.

LOTS-OF-MUFFINS

This should give you 2½ dozen muffins. They're great served hot with a butterscotch sauce as a dessert.

> 1 cup butter or margarine
> 1 cup brown sugar
> 1 egg
> 1 teaspoon vanilla
> ½ cup molasses or corn syrup
> 3 cups flour
> 1 teaspoon baking soda
> ½ teaspoon cinnamon
> ½ teaspoon ground cloves
> 1½ cups milk
> ¾ cup raisins, chopped dates, or walnuts

Cream the butter and sugar; beat in egg, vanilla, and molasses. Add the sifted dry ingredients alternately with the milk. Stir in the raisins. Spoon batter into 30 buttered and floured muffin cups, and bake at 350°F for 25 minutes. Turn out on a rack and serve hot.

PEANUT BUTTER MUFFINS

Peanut butter freaks will love these. Let your growing boys try them.

½ cup peanut butter
3 tablespoons vegetable oil
¼ cup sugar, brown or white
1 teaspoon salt
1 egg
1½ cups milk
1 cup all-purpose flour
1 tablespoon baking powder
1 cup whole-wheat flour
Peanut butter to spoon on top

Blend the peanut butter and oil. Add the sugar and salt; beat in the egg, stir in the milk. Sift the white flour and baking powder into a bowl, stir in the whole-wheat flour, then combine with the peanut butter mixture just enough to completely moisten the flour. Spoon into buttered muffin tins. Put about 1 teaspoonful of peanut butter on top of each muffin. Bake at 400°F for 20 minutes. Spread the hot peanut butter over the muffin — quite a nice touch.

SQUASH OR PUMPKIN MUFFINS

Crisp on the outside, tender inside, and golden throughout. You can give these more texture by adding ½ cup of toasted, shelled pumpkin seeds or sunflower seeds, or chopped walnuts or dates.

⅔ cup cooked puréed pumpkin or squash
½ cup milk, light cream, or commercial sour cream
¼ cup oil, or melted butter or margarine
1 egg, beaten
1¾ cups flour
2 teaspoons baking powder
½ teaspoon baking soda
Pinch of salt
½ teaspoon cinnamon
½ teaspoon nutmeg
¼ teaspoon ginger

Blend well the pumpkin, milk, oil, and egg. Into the liquid mixture sift the flour, baking powder, baking soda, salt, and spices — and any other ingredients you care to add. Fold together gently until just mixed, then spoon into buttered muffin tins and bake at 400°F for about 20 minutes. Cool only slightly on a rack before you serve them. Softened cream cheese spread over them gives them a nice touch.

Buttermilk and Sour Milk

Many of my mother's recipes and those of my friend Bevvy Martin, who gave me many Old Order Mennonite recipes, call for sour milk. The recipes in my books list buttermilk instead of sour milk because they are interchangeable. Unless you have a cow, you can no longer get natural sour milk. Milk that you buy must be pasteurized and it doesn't clabber; it just gets bad and unusable.

I like baking with buttermilk; I always keep some in my fridge where it would keep for months if I didn't use it. I think it adds flavour to muffins and quick breads and cakes. Whenever I get a new cookbook I go through it and write a large B beside the title of a recipe that uses buttermilk. Those are the recipes I usually try first.

You can make your own buttermilk! Because commercial buttermilk is merely milk with a culture added to give it flavour and a heavier consistency, you can add ½ cup of commercial buttermilk to a quart of milk — both at room temperature. Add ½ teaspoon salt, stir well and cover it. Let it stand in your kitchen until it has clabbered, then put it in your fridge until you are ready to make lots of super muffins and quick breads or anything else that requires it.

If you are an impulsive baker and haven't planned far enough ahead, you can clabber milk more quickly by adding 1 tablespoon of white vinegar or lemon juice to enough room-temperature milk to make 1 cup. Let it stand 5 to 10 minutes — or until it clabbers. I never do this because I like buttermilk better and I always have some on hand.

SEVEN GRAIN CEREAL MUFFINS

Harold Horwood, Newfoundland's leading author, spoke at the Kitchener Public Library one freezing rainy day. While he was driving and walking on the ice to my cottage, I put these muffins in the oven. With Dubonnet and pieces of cheese we both ate four, and he took the rest home to Corky, his wife.

1 cup 7-grain cereal or Red River cereal
1 cup buttermilk
½ cup oil
½ cup brown sugar
1 cup raisins
1 teaspoon salt
1 cup flour (I used whole-wheat)
1 teaspoon baking powder
½ teaspoon baking soda
2 teaspoons ginger
½ teaspoon cinnamon

Put the cereal into a bowl, pour the buttermilk over it, add the oil, sugar, raisins, and salt; mix them and let rest for about half an hour, unless you are in a rush. Sift the flour, baking powder, baking soda, ginger, and cinnamon into the cereal mixture; stir just enough to dampen all the flour, adding a bit more milk if you need to. Spoon into greased muffin tins; it will make a dozen fat ones. Bake in a 400°F oven about 20 minutes and eat them hot, hot. The cereal I used had hard crunchy bits in it but the texture of the muffins was light as a feather. Harold told me he uses molasses instead of sugar in all his muffins.

ORANGE RAISIN MUFFINS

For after-church company in Bevvy Martin's house.

2 cups flour
⅓ cup sugar
¾ teaspoon baking soda
½ teaspoon salt
½ cup raisins
1 egg, well beaten
⅓ cup orange juice
½ teaspoon grated orange rind
⅔ cup buttermilk
⅓ cup shortening, melted

Sift together the flour, sugar, baking soda, and salt; add the raisins. Combine the egg, orange juice, rind, buttermilk, and melted shortening. Turn wet ingredients into the dry and mix only until dry ones are dampened. Fill greased muffin tins two-thirds full. Bake in a 400°F oven for about 20 to 30 minutes. Keep your eye on them.

STRAWBERRY BUTTER

This is a very special treat you can make during the strawberry season to spread on hot muffins, toast, or biscuits.

2 or 3 ripe strawberries — the number depends
on the ripeness and size
½ cup softened butter
1 teaspoon lemon juice

Crush the berries and beat them into the softened butter with the lemon juice until smooth. That's it. Store in a pretty little pottery jar with a lid in your fridge or spread it on wax paper and shape it into a roll 1½ inches in diameter. If the mixture is too soft, chill it before shaping. Store the roll in fridge and cut in slices to spread.

Fruit Muffins

Your phone rings in the afternoon and a friend says, "Put the kettle on, dear. We'll be with you in half an hour for a cup of tea."

"Great," you answer, "I'll be so glad to see you," and you mean it but you're also frantically thinking, "What in the world can I feed them?"

The answer is MUFFINS: *quick, easy, delicious, and foolproof, made with ingredients you have in your cupboard.*

Turn on the oven. Give your muffin tins a good buttering, sift the dry ingredients into a bowl, blend the liquids, mix them together with a few strokes of a spoon. Drop the batter into the tins, put them in the hot oven for 20 minutes while you tidy up and listen for the timer that tells you the muffins are baked.

As your friends come in the door, they'll say, "Wow! Something smells good in here."

Muffins loaded with fruit, fresh, frozen, canned, or jam, will be remembered forever.

APPLE, CARROT, AND WALNUT MUFFINS

A lady who said she was raised like a princess in India said these were the best muffins she had ever tasted. I wouldn't be quite so enthusiastic myself, but they are pretty good. A food processor makes the grating much easier.

> **2 cups grated apple**
> **1 cup grated carrot (use your food processor)**
> **2 eggs**
> **½ cup sugar**
> **½ cup oil**
> **1 teaspoon almond flavouring**
> **1 cup whole-wheat flour**
> **1 cup all-purpose flour**
> **1 tablespoon baking powder**
> **½ teaspoon baking soda**
> **½ teaspoon cinnamon**
> **½ cup chopped walnuts**
> **Walnut halves**

Combine apple, carrot, eggs, sugar, oil, and flavouring. In another bowl, combine flours, baking powder, baking soda, cinnamon, and chopped walnuts. Add the apple-carrot mixture to the flour mixture. Stir until they are just combined. Spoon batter into 24 buttered and floured muffin cups and put a walnut on top for decoration. Bake at 375°F for 25 minutes. Remove to a rack and serve hot.

RUBY'S FRESH APPLE-CINNAMON MUFFINS

Moist, tender, and very tasty.

1½ cups flour
¼ cup instant skim-milk powder
⅓ cup sugar
2 teaspoons baking powder
1 teaspoon baking soda
½ teaspoon cinnamon
½ teaspoon salt
1 egg
½ cup water
¼ cup melted butter or oil
1 cup finely chopped apple

Topping:
¼ cup brown sugar
⅓ cup chopped nuts
½ teaspoon cinnamon

Combine flour, skim-milk powder, sugar, baking powder, baking soda, cinnamon, and salt. Beat egg with water. Stir in butter and apple. Add apple mixture all at once to flour mixture. Stir only till moistened. Pour into 12 buttered and floured muffin cups.

Combine topping ingredients. Sprinkle on muffins. Bake at 375°F for 20 to 25 minutes. Remove immediately to a rack and serve warm.

If you prefer, you may use regular milk instead of powdered. But if, like me, you live in the country — and without a cow — you might want to save yourself a trip to the store by using powdered milk in your baking.

VERY RIPE BANANA MUFFINS

Delicate, tasty and tender

> **3 ripe bananas (1 cupful mashed)**
> **⅓ cup melted shortening or oil**
> **½ cup sugar**
> **1 teaspoon salt**
> **1 egg, well beaten**
> **1 teaspoon vanilla**
> **1½ cups flour**
> **1 teaspoon baking powder**
> **½ teaspoon baking soda**
> **½ cup chopped walnuts(optional)**

Mash the bananas, add the shortening, sugar, and salt; beat till they blend. Add the egg and vanilla and beat again. (You may do that much in your mixer or blender if you like, but no more.) Sift the flour, baking powder, and baking soda into the banana mixture, add the nuts, stir with a few strokes of your spatula or spoon — only enough to moisten the flour. Drop spoonfuls into greased muffin tins and bake in a 350°F oven for 15 or 20 minutes. You should have 18 muffins. Tip the muffins onto a rack to cool only slightly before you gobble them with that cup of tea.

BANANA COCONUT MUFFINS

Coconut is nice with bananas; try adding ½ cup shredded or flaked coconut to the recipe.

CARROT BANANA MUFFINS

Use only ½ cup bananas and add **1 cup finely grated carrots**. Add a **pinch of spice** if you like — cinnamon, nutmeg, cloves — or a blend.

RUBY'S BANANA ROLLED-OAT MUFFINS

When bananas are on sale at the supermarket I usually buy more than I can use. When they begin to get soft, I put the surplus into my freezer, each banana tucked in wherever it fits. Then when I want to bake banana muffins or bread or cake, I find them, let them thaw slightly and scrape them out of their skins. The banana flavour is very strong.

> **1 cup mashed banana (2 or 3 bananas)**
> **½ cup milk**
> **½ cup rolled oats**
> **1 cup flour**
> **½ cup sugar**
> **1 tablespoon baking powder**
> **½ teaspoon baking soda**
> **½ teaspoon salt**
> **½ teaspoon cinnamon**
> **¼ teaspoon nutmeg**
> **⅓ cup melted shortening or oil**
> **1 egg**
> **1 teaspoon vanilla**

Smash the bananas until they are liquified. Add the milk and rolled oats. Let stand while you sift the dry ingredients into a bowl. Blend the shortening, egg, and vanilla with the rolled-oat mixture. Pour it into the dry ingredients. Stir just enough to moisten all the flour. Fill 12 greased muffin cups, and bake at 375°F for about 20 minutes.

NORM'S BLUEBERRY MUFFINS

I've eaten a lot of blueberry muffins in my day, but none as good as these.

¼ cup butter (and Norm uses butter)
¾ cup sugar
1 egg, well beaten
1½ cups pastry flour
2 teaspoons baking powder
½ teaspoon salt
½ cup milk
1 cup blueberries, fresh or frozen

Cream the butter and sugar, add the egg and beat till creamy. Add the sifted dry ingredients alternately with the milk. Lightly fold in the berries. Drop into buttered muffin tins. Bake at 375°F for 15 to 20 minutes, and you'll have a dozen super-stars!

SUMMER BERRY MUFFINS

Instead of blueberries fold in 1 cup of whatever berries are in season: rhubarb, strawberries, raspberries, currants; if large, cut to the size of a raspberry. Some berries tend to turn the batter gray, but they taste good.

SURPRISE MUFFINS

Half fill buttered muffin tins with blueberry muffin batter (without the blueberries); drop in a rounded teaspoon of **jam or a piece of fruit** (half-thawed raspberries are great). Cover with the rest of the batter and bake at 350°F for 18 to 20 minutes.

CITRUS MUFFINS

You can use a small grapefruit or a large orange to make these light, luscious muffins to enjoy with your tea.

1 grapefruit, or large orange
1 egg
½ cup additional grapefruit or orange juice
   (fresh or powdered crystals and water)
½ cup butter or margarine
1½ cups flour
½ cup sugar
1 teaspoon baking powder
1 teaspoon baking soda

Topping (optional):
¼ cup sugar
1 teaspoon cinnamon
Chopped walnuts, sunflower seeds,
   coconut, chopped dates, or raisins

Cut the fruit into 6 to 8 pieces. Remove pips. Put fruit pieces in food processor. (If you haven't a food processor, heaven help you, because the fruit must be chopped *fine.*) Drop in egg, juice and butter. Blend until the butter chunks have disappeared and the whole mixture looks like scrambled eggs. Sift the dry ingredients into a bowl. Stir in the orange mixture just enough to moisten. Spoon the batter into 18 buttered and floured muffin cups. Sprinkle with the mixed topping. Bake at 400°F about 20 minutes. Turn out on a rack and serve warm.

CRANBERRY SAUCE MUFFINS

For quite a while I had half a jar of cranberry sauce taking up space in my fridge. These muffins were a good solution for getting rid of it. Very pretty and tasty, too.

2 cups flour
½ cup sugar
1 tablespoon baking powder
½ teaspoon salt
1 cup or less cranberry sauce
¼ cup oil
1 egg
1 cup milk

In a large bowl, sift together the flour, sugar, baking powder, and salt. In another bowl, beat the oil and egg slightly. Stir in the cranberry sauce. Stir in the milk and pour into the flour mixture. Stir until just moistened. Drop batter into well-buttered muffin tins — about 18 — and bake in a 400°F oven for 20 minutes. Tip onto a rack and eat them hot.

BERRY JAM MUFFINS

You could try this recipe with any jam that has whole berries in place of the cranberry sauce.

MINCE MUFFINS

At Christmas time when you have some **mince** in the house, you might try using a cupful in your muffins. Put a **candied cherry** on top for the season.

LEMON MUFFINS

These tart little muffins are ideal to serve with a fruit salad.

½ cup butter or margarine
¼ cup sugar
2 eggs, separated
1 cup flour
1 teaspoon baking powder
Pinch of salt
¼ cup concentrate for lemonade (thawed)

Cream the butter and sugar together until light; beat in the well-beaten egg yolks. Lightly stir in the sifted dry ingredients alternately with the lemon concentrate. Beat the egg whites until stiff and fold in gently. Spoon into small buttered muffin cups and bake at 375°F for about 20 minutes.

DATE AND ORANGE MUFFINS

These are my sister Ruby's favourite muffins. And no wonder.

1 whole orange
½ cup orange juice
½ cup chopped dates
1 egg
½ cup butter or margarine
1½ cups flour
1 teaspoon baking soda
1 teaspoon baking powder
⅔ cup white sugar
1 teaspoon salt

Cut the whole orange into pieces to remove the seeds. Drop the pieces into the blender or food processor with the ½ cup orange juice and whirl till the peel is finely chopped. Drop in the dates, egg, and butter; give them a very short whirl. Into a bowl sift the flour, baking soda, baking powder, sugar, and salt. Pour the orange mixture over the dry, stir lightly, just enough to moisten. Drop spoonfuls into buttered muffin tins and bake at 400°F for about 15 minutes. They are super.

MY OWN PLUM MUFFINS

Tart and tasty, not ordinary muffins, these are rather special.

2 cups flour
2½ teaspoons baking powder
1 teaspoon salt
1¼ cups sugar
½ cup chopped nuts
1 cup chopped up plums
1 egg, lightly beaten
¾ cup milk
Grated orange or grapefruit rind
¼ cup oil
⅛ teaspoon cinnamon

Sift the flour, baking powder, salt, and 1 cup of the sugar. Stir in the nuts, then the plums. Blend the egg, milk, rind, and oil. Pour into dry ingredients and stir only until flour is moistened, no more. Spoon the batter into 12 buttered muffin tins. Stir a bit of cinnamon into remaining ¼ cup sugar and sprinkle over muffins. Bake at 400°F for 20 minutes.

RHUBARB MUFFINS

Crisp on the outside, tender and moist on the inside; these freeze well — if they last long enough.

1 egg
1 cup brown sugar
½ cup shortening
1 teaspoon salt
1 cup buttermilk
1½ cups diced rhubarb
2 cups flour
1 teaspoon baking soda
1 teaspoon cinnamon

Beat the egg. Beat in brown sugar, shortening, and salt. Stir in buttermilk, then rhubarb. Sift flour, baking soda, and cinnamon together into the mixture. Stir only until all the flour is moistened. Spoon into 12 buttered and floured muffin cups, and bake at 375°F for 20 minutes. You can make these with frozen rhubarb, as well — baking them a bit longer.

PEACH MUFFINS

Plump, tender and delicious — absolutely marvellous — these should be eaten on the day they are baked. Lorna's husband, Ross, who never eats more than one of anything said, "Do you realize we have each eaten three?"

>   1½ cups flour
>   1½ teaspoons baking powder
>   1 teaspoon salt
>   ¼ cup white sugar
>   ¼ cup brown sugar
>   1 large egg
>   ½ cup milk
>   ¼ cup melted butter or vegetable oil
>   1 teaspoon almond flavouring
>   1½ cups fresh, sliced peaches
>   (you don't need to peel them)
>   White or powdered sugar for topping

Sift the flour, baking powder, and salt into a bowl; stir in the sugar. Beat the egg, add the milk, shortening, and almond flavouring, beating all together. Pour the egg mixture over the dry ingredients, stir until barely moistened, then lightly fold in the sliced peaches. Drop spoonfuls into well-buttered muffin tins. Bake in a 400°F oven for about 20 minutes, or until golden. Dip the tops into powdered sugar while hot and serve before they cool.

If you think some might be left over or if you want to freeze them, dissolve 2 teaspoons of Fruit Keep in 3 tablespoons of water, stir in the sliced peaches to coat them and drain well before adding them to the muffin mixture. If you don't, the peaches will turn brown and their flavour is medicinal. Too bad.

MARNIE'S TEA PARTY

When I visited Marnie Paisley at her winter home near Tucson, Arizona, she invited sixteen ladies for afternoon tea. In the morning we made four kinds of muffins for the event. I didn't have my muffin recipes with me and had to guess what to put in them; I must have guessed right: all the ladies wanted all the recipes.

ORANGE AND GRAPEFRUIT PEEL MUFFINS

These were the hit of the day: bitter-sweet, made with the peel of a grapefruit and an orange that Marnie and I had for breakfast.

Peel of 1 grapefruit and 1 orange
1 to 2 cups buttermilk
1 cup sugar
1 teaspoon salt
½ cup shortening
2 cups flour
2 teaspoons baking powder
½ teaspoon baking soda

Cut up the complete grapefruit and / or orange skins into your blender or food processor, pour in the buttermilk and whirl till the skin is finely ground. Add the sugar, salt, and shortening; the mixture will be a mush. Into a bowl sift the dry ingredients. Pour the rind mixture over the flour and stir just enough to blend — you may need more buttermilk. Spoon into buttered muffin tins and bake in a 400°F oven for 20 minutes. They'll be light, have great flavour, will stay moist, reheat well, and freeze perfectly.

APPLE CINNAMON MUFFINS

This was my recollection of my sister Ruby's Fresh Apple Cinnamon Muffins — not quite the same but very moist and refreshing. The ladies liked these, too. Marnie served pieces of cheese along with them.

½ cup margarine or butter
¾ cup sugar
1 egg, beaten
1 cup buttermilk
1 teaspoon salt
1½ cups unpeeled, sliced apple
2 cups flour — 1 whole-wheat, 1 white
1 teaspoon baking soda
1 teaspoon cinnamon

Topping:
1 teaspoon cinnamon
2 or 3 tablespoons sugar

Blend the margarine, sugar, and beaten egg till smooth; add the buttermilk, salt, and sliced apples, mixing well. Add the flour, baking soda, cinnamon, sifted together, and stir just enough to moisten. Spoon into buttered muffin cups (at Marnie's we used small ones), sprinkle with cinnamon and sugar mixed together, and bake at 400°F for 20 minutes

RUBY'S OATMEAL MUFFINS

At Marnie's I put dates in these and they weren't quite as light and buttery as when I make them without but they were still very popular.

1 cup rolled oats
1 cup buttermilk
1 cup flour
1 teaspoon salt
½ teaspoon baking soda
1½ teaspoons baking powder
½ cup melted shortening or oil

½ cup brown sugar
1 egg, beaten
1 teaspoon vanilla
1 cup chopped dates (optional)

Combine the oats and buttermilk, let soak while you heat your oven, butter your pans, assemble and mix all your other ingredients. Sift the flour with the salt, baking soda, and baking powder. To the oatmeal mixture add the melted shortening, brown sugar, beaten egg, vanilla, and dates. Pour in the sifted dry ingredients and stir only long enough to moisten. Spoon into buttered muffin pans and bake at 400°F for 15 to 20 minutes, until golden. Eat while they are hot.

MAPLE CORNMEAL MUFFINS

This neat little muffin rises up and looks like a Mexican hat. It has a delicate maple flavour and needs no embellishment.

2 eggs
⅔ cup milk
⅓ cup maple syrup
½ cup melted shortening or oil
1⅓ cups flour
⅔ cup cornmeal
3 teaspoons baking powder
½ teaspoon salt

Beat the eggs. Add milk, syrup, and shortening; mix well. Add the dry ingredients sifted together and blend just enough to moisten. Spoon into 12 greased muffin tins and bake at 400°F for 20 minutes. They will be golden and crusty.

Bran Muffins

One day I was shopping along the main street in Elmira, I saw a great sack of pretzels in the window of Brubacher's 1890's grocery store (which is no longer in existence).

"Why do you have so many?" I asked frisky old Noah Brubacher.

"The Mennonite ladies like to eat them at their quiltings. Since pretzels are dry, the ladies' fingers don't get sticky or greasy and soil the quilts while they're sewing."

I bought a bagful, then wondered when I got home what I would do with them. If I have nibbly things in my house I'm tempted to eat them between meals, which of course I shouldn't do. I must incorporate them in a meal. I love crackers and cheese, why not pretzels and cheese? At the time I had a pound of good, ripe, tender limburger cheese which I'd carefully sealed in a jar for obvious olfactory reasons. Next morning I ate pretzels and limburger for my breakfast. It was so superior that when I had none left I bought more. I ate limburger for breakfast all fall and winter.

In April I was asked to speak to a small group of senior citizens. When I arrived at the meeting place, instead of a group of perhaps twenty-five, there was a hall full of people — at least two hundred. They sat with notebooks and pencils poised and they weren't just seniors.

I told them I wasn't going to give them recipes. I was invited to tell senior citizens what I ate to keep healthy while living alone. I told them I started my day with pretzels and limburger.

Next day there was a picture of me in the Waterloo Chronicle *with a headline, "Author eats pretzels and limburger cheese for breakfast." I hadn't known there was a reporter at the meeting.*

I laughed at the headline but my sister was furious; she said, "It's bad enough that you eat pretzels and limburger for breakfast but it's worse having you tell that you do it."

I no longer do it. When I went on a motor trip to California with my sister and her husband and indulged my limburger-pretzel passion every morning, they convinced me that pretzels have too much salt and ripe limburger on a trip can be obnoxious. What a pity.

Since then I have been eating bran muffins for breakfast and I must admit it is an improvement — in my morale, my health, and in public and family relations.

EVERY MORNING BRAN MUFFINS

No eggs, no shortening: these have a crisp, chewy outside and soft inside. They're easy to make and taste good, too. I bake mine in my little toaster oven.

1 cup bran
1 cup raisins or chopped dates
1 cup milk
½ teaspoon salt
½ cup brown sugar
1 cup flour
2 teaspoons baking powder
1 teaspoon cinnamon

Mix together the bran, raisins, milk, salt, and sugar. Let stand for a while — an hour is preferable but 30 minutes will do — or overnight. Sift dry ingredients together into the wet mixture, and stir just enough to moisten. Spoon batter into 12 buttered and floured muffin cups. Bake at 400°F for about 20 minutes. Keep them in the fridge and warm one or two every morning for breakfast. You'll be joyful all day.

BANANA BRAN MUFFINS

Slices of **banana** stirred into bran muffins, instead of raisins, make a nice change.

JAM BRAN MUFFINS

Sometimes I have some jam that needs finishing up and I make these muffins to get rid of it. I never throw anything out.

½ cup margarine or ⅓ cup oil
1 cup brown sugar
1 egg
2 tablespoons molasses
1 cup buttermilk
1½ cups bran
1 cup flour
1 teaspoon baking soda
½ teaspoon cinnamon
1 rounded teaspoon jam for each muffin
Sugar for topping
Cinnamon for topping

Blend the margarine and sugar, then add the egg, molasses, and buttermilk. Stir in the bran and let the mixture rest for a while. Sift together the flour, soda, and cinnamon. Stir the two mixtures together until just blended. Put a tablespoonful of the batter into each of 12 buttered and floured muffin cups. Place a teaspoon of jam in each cup, then fill the cups with the rest of the batter. Sprinkle each muffin with a mixture of white sugar and cinnamon, and bake at 400°F for 20 minutes. Remove to a rack and eat warm.

JEAN SALTER'S BRAN MUFFINS AND BRAN LOAF

Without eggs or shortening, the outside is chewy, the inside moist and delicious. Jean has these for breakfast every day and she doesn't gain weight.

> **1 cup bran**
> **1 cup mixed dried fruit or raisins**
> **1 cup milk**
> **1 cup brown sugar**
> **1 cup flour**
> **1 teaspoon baking powder**

Mix together first four ingredients and soak for 1 hour, if you can wait that long. Add flour and baking powder and stir to combine. Spoon into buttered muffin tins and bake at 350°F for about 20 minutes.

For the Bran Loaf spread the batter in a buttered loaf pan and bake at 350°F for about 40 minutes. Test it.

BREAKFAST BRAN MUFFINS

These are great with butter and jam: crusty on the outside and tender inside. Try them with or without an egg in the batter to vary the texture.

> **2 cups flour**
> **2 tablespoons sugar**
> **1 tablespoon baking powder**
> **½ teaspoon salt**
> **1 cup bran**
> **3 tablespoons shortening or oil**
> **1 cup buttermilk**
> **1 or 2 eggs (optional)**
> **1 cup raisins (optional)**

Sift and mix all the dry ingredients. Cut in the shortening — unless you use oil, which can be blended with the buttermilk and egg. Add buttermilk mixture to bran mixture and stir just enough to moisten. Stir in raisins. Spoon into 12 buttered and floured muffin cups, and bake at 375°F for about 25 minutes.

BRAN GEMS

These light and tender ones are good any time of the day. One day a woman called me from Montreal; she said she had searched all over the city for gem pans and nobody knew what they were. It's the old-fashioned word for muffin tins.

1 cup whole-wheat or all-purpose flour
1 cup bran
¼ cup wheat germ
1 cup brown sugar (or half molasses)
¾ teaspoon salt
1 teaspoon baking powder
1 egg
½ cup oil or shortening
½ cup milk
1 teaspoon vanilla
½ cup raisins or chopped dates

Thoroughly mix all the dry ingredients; blend the egg, oil, milk, and vanilla. Pour the wet into the dry mixture, add raisins or dates and stir till just combined. Half fill 18 greased gem pans (or muffin tins) and bake at 375°F for about 20 minutes. Cool on a rack.

HEALTHY HONEY-BRAN MUFFINS

Grated orange rind gives these a distinctive flavour.

¼ cup butter or margarine
⅓ cup honey
1 egg
1 cup buttermilk
Grated rind of 1 or 2 oranges
1 cup flour
1 teaspoon baking soda
¼ teaspoon salt
1 cup bran
½ cup or more raisins or chopped dates

Melt the butter and honey together. Beat in the egg and buttermilk with grated rind. Sift together the flour, baking soda, and salt. Stir in the bran and raisins, then the buttermilk mixture. Blend just enough to moisten. Spoon into 12 large or 18 medium well-buttered and floured muffin cups. Bake at 350°F for 20 minutes. Remove muffins to a rack and eat warm.

WALNUT, DATE, AND RAISIN BRAN MUFFINS

Though there is no butter in them, these have a buttery taste.

> **1 egg, slightly beaten**
> **⅓ cup brown sugar**
> **3 tablespoons molasses**
> **½ cup oil**
> **1 teaspoon vanilla**
> **1⅓ cups buttermilk**
> **1½ cups bran**
> **⅓ cup chopped dates**
> **⅓ cup raisins**
> **⅓ cup chopped walnuts**
> **⅔ cup flour**
> **⅔ cup whole-wheat flour**
> **2 teaspoons baking powder**
> **1¼ teaspoons baking soda**

Combine egg, sugar, molasses, oil, vanilla, buttermilk, bran, dates, raisins, and walnuts. Sift dry ingredients into wet mixture, stirring just enough to moisten. Spoon batter into 18 buttered and floured muffin cups. Bake at 400°F for 20 minutes. Remove muffins from pans to a rack. Serve hot.

APPLE AND CIDER BRAN MUFFINS

Janet Berton said, "These are the best muffins I have ever eaten in my life." She had just arrived at my cottage after being lost for an hour trying to find my place in the wilderness of Waterloo region. But she said the same thing the next morning when she had the muffins for breakfast.

1 egg
½ cup brown sugar
½ cup oil
¼ cup molasses
¾ cup sweet cider
2 medium apples, chopped
1½ cups flour
¾ cup bran
1 tablespoon baking powder
1 teaspoon baking soda
½ teaspoon salt
½ teaspoon nutmeg
½ cup chopped walnuts
1 cup raisins

Combine the egg, sugar, oil, and molasses. Add the cider and the chopped apple. (If you have a food processor, simply drop the apple pieces into the bowl and give it a whirl.) Sift the dry ingredients into a bowl. Stir in the nuts and raisins. Then add the apple mixture and stir until the flour is just moistened. Spoon batter into 24 buttered and floured muffin cups, and bake at 400°F for 15 to 20 minutes. Turn out of the pan on a rack and leave until cool enough to hold in your hand.

JACK'S OAT-BRAN MUFFINS

Recently, scientific tests have proved that eating oat bran may reduce cholesterol in food. Jack Hutchinson, who has a cottage on Sunfish Lake, eats two oat-bran muffins every day and no longer worries about cholesterol. Of course he avoids rich fatty foods as well.

2 cups oat bran
⅓ cup flour
2 tablespoons brown sugar
¼ cup chopped nuts
½ cup raisins
1 tablespoon baking powder
½ teaspoon salt
¼ teaspoon cinnamon
¾ cup milk
2 eggs, beaten
⅓ cup honey or molasses
2 tablespoons vegetable oil

In a bowl, stir together oat bran, flour, brown sugar, nuts, raisins, baking powder, salt, and cinnamon. In another bowl, mix together milk, eggs, honey, and oil. Pour the liquid ingredients into the dry ones. Mix just enough to moisten, then spoon batter into 12 greased muffin cups. Bake at 400°F for about 20 minutes.

SPICY OAT-BRAN MUFFINS

These are made without sugar and have an old-fashioned mo-lasses taste.

> **1 egg, beaten**
> **¼ cup oil**
> **⅓ cup molasses**
> **¾ cup milk**
> **1¼ cups flour**
> **¾ cup oat bran**
> **2 teaspoons baking powder**
> **½ teaspoon cinnamon**
> **½ teaspoon nutmeg**
> **½ teaspoon salt**
> **1 cup raisins or chopped dates (optional)**

Mix together egg, oil, molasses, and milk. Combine flour, oat bran, baking powder, cinnamon, nutmeg, salt, and raisins. Stir in the egg mixture quickly until just combined. Do not overmix. Fill 12 greased muffin cups, and bake in a 375°F oven for 15 to 18 minutes. Serve warm.

MY OAT-BRAN MUFFINS

One day when Elsie and Anne came for tea, I made these muffins with oat bran; the batter was runny — as it shouldn't have been. When I tapped the baked muffins onto a rack, the lower halves didn't come out of the tins until I scraped them out with a knife. The result was a mass of crumbs, pieces, crisp edges and tops. I served the "muffins" in my Pink Tower Spode soup dishes with dessert spoons. The three of us ate one and a half dozen — but in their crumbled state it didn't seem like so many.

> 1 teaspoon baking soda
> 1 cup buttermilk
> ¼ teaspoon salt
> 1 cup brown sugar
> 1 egg
> Dollop of molasses (about 2 tablespoons
>   if you're fussy enough to measure)
> 1 cup oat bran
> 1 cup raisins
> 1 cup flour
> 1 teaspoon baking powder
> Sugar for topping
> Cinnamon for topping

Sprinkle baking soda over buttermilk and let stand while you mix the salt, sugar, egg, molasses, bran, and raisins. Stir in the buttermilk then the flour and baking powder sifted together. Spoon into 18 well-buttered and floured muffin cups. Sprinkle each muffin with a couple of pinches of sugar and cinnamon blended together before you put the tins into the oven. Bake at 400°F for 20 minutes.

If you don't like your muffins crumbly, you might make these with wheat bran which absorbs moisture or put in more flour to make a stiffer batter.

DATE BRAN MUFFINS

Tender, tasty and functional, these are easy to whip up in a hurry. No eggs. Anne Spencer could eat half of these at a sitting. So could I.

> 1 cup chopped dates
> 1 cup brown sugar
> ½ cup melted shortening or oil
> 1 cup buttermilk
> ¼ teaspoon salt
> 1 cup bran
> 1 cup flour
> 1 teaspoon baking soda
> 1 teaspoon baking powder
> 1 teaspoon cinnamon

Mix ingredients together in the order given, stirring no longer than needed to moisten the flour. Spoon into 18 buttered and floured muffin cups, and bake at 425° for 15 minutes. Remove to a rack and eat hot.

Company Muffins

Whenever I have been asked to give something to a fund-raising auction, I have promised "Tea and Muffins for Six" at my cottage on Sunfish Lake. The bidding has gone from $65 to $200 — an exorbitant price to pay for tea and muffins. But the money is always donated to a good cause — and I do give up a whole day of my working time.

Whoever won the bid was supposed to call me to set a date, but I never heard from the Writers' Union of Canada bidders who lived in Ottawa, Edmonton, and Toronto.

Two of the Kitchener-Waterloo Art Gallery members who won the bid were acquaintances who had several times invited me to elegant parties — hospitality I had never returned. And they paid $140 to come to my cottage for tea and muffins!

Several times people shared the bid; I made muffins and we had a pleasant afternoon — at least I did and they said they did.

This summer five young career women, all strangers, were coming from Cambridge. I made muffins all morning. First I made Orange Raisin Muffins (page 11) but used frozen orange concentrate instead of orange juice. As I was putting the batter into the pans I realized — too late — that I'd forgotten the raisins. The muffins when they came out of the oven were thin and flat with a hole in the centre as if they'd been poked by a finger.

To use the plumped-up but forgotten raisins I decided next to make Walnut, Date, and Raisin Bran Muffins (page 32).

I started mixing the liquids, went to my back bedroom where I store my staples, and couldn't find any bran. I used oat bran instead of wheat bran — though I should have known better from past experience (page 36). When I turned the baked muffins onto a rack the tops came out, but the rest stayed in the pans and I had to scrape them out with a spoon. Second disaster. I kept eating the crumbs and bits of top — enough for two dozen muffins which, of course, I couldn't allow to be wasted. I put the crumbs into a bowl, beat an egg with some milk and poured it over the crumbs. I washed and rebuttered the muffin tins, filled them with the muffin crumb mixture and put them back in the hot oven for 15 minutes. The resulting "muffins" looked a bit ragged, were quite heavy, but had a great taste — rather like plum pudding, the ladies said.

Time for me was running out. The ladies were coming at two o'clock. I decided I must make my third batch with a recipe I knew was foolproof. Maple Syrup Muffins (page 41) have never failed. The batter I made was thicker than it should have been, but because I was in a rush I dropped it into the tins and put them in the oven while I quickly dressed up for my company. The muffins came out fine. They looked more like tea biscuits than muffins, but no matter.

The five ladies arrived. If I'd just been serving a friend or two, I'd have dropped a bit of marmalade into the holes in the Orange Muffins after I'd reheated them but with five strangers in my summer-room I couldn't stay in my kitchen fiddling around filling up holes. I had to get the muffins out and into my guests.

When I confessed my failures, they were tolerant and pleasant. One said, "It makes me feel good to know that your baking, like mine, doesn't always turn out well."

A week later three Dares and their wives were coming to have tea and muffins. The Dares own Dare Foods Limited, a great cookie factory which turns out delicious perfect cookies by the millions and sends them all over the world.

I chose to make muffins that have never failed me: Ginger Raisin (page 40), Maple Syrup with a glaze (page 41), and Apple Butter (page 42). And I followed the recipes exactly.

The muffins behaved very well. The Dares arrived and enthusiastically ate three or four muffins apiece, while we chatted all afternoon about my involvement in the Great Cookie War (which I described in my book Schmecks Appeal).

GINGER RAISIN MUFFINS

One day when four friends were coming to my cottage I didn't have an egg to put in my muffins, so I had to invent some without eggs. My male guest ate four, the ladies two apiece — and they were fat ones (I mean the muffins).

> ½ cup shortening (I used margarine)
> ½ cup packed brown sugar
> 1 teaspoon salt
> ½ cup milk
> ½ cup molasses, blended with the milk
> 1 cup whole-wheat flour
> 1 cup all-purpose flour
> 1 tablespoon baking powder
> 2 teaspoons ginger
> ½ teaspoon cinnamon
> ½ teaspoon nutmeg
> 1 cup raisins

Cream the shortening with the sugar and salt, blend with the milk and molasses. Stir together the flours, baking powder, ginger, cinnamon, and nutmeg. Pour the liquid ingredients over the dry — or the dry into the liquid — drop in the raisins, and stir just enough to moisten the flour. Spoon into the well-buttered muffin tins and bake at 400°F for about 20 minutes. Serve warm.

MAPLE SYRUP MUFFINS

These glazed muffins look company-fancy; they're light as angel food and their flavour is divine.

¼ cup shortening, margarine is fine
½ cup sugar
1 teaspoon salt
1½ cups flour
1 tablespoon baking powder
¾ cup rolled oats
½ cup milk
½ cup maple syrup

Glaze:
1 tablespoon butter
½ cup icing sugar
1 tablespoon maple syrup, or a bit more

Soften the shortening, blend in the sugar and salt; add the flour sifted with the baking powder and blend with a pastry cutter till the mixture is crumbly (I use my food processor); mix in the rolled oats. Blend the milk and syrup together in a measuring cup, pour the mixture over the dry ingredients and stir just enough to moisten. Drop into muffin tins and bake at 350°F for 20 minutes.

While they are baking, combine the glaze ingredients and spread over the muffins when they come out of the oven and have cooled just a little bit. Serve them warm. Your guests will apologize for being such gluttons — but no one can resist these.

APPLE BUTTER MUFFINS

When Elsie brought a friend out for tea one day, they each ate two muffins and asked if they could take a third one home with them. Of course. With apple butter slathered on top after they have been reheated, these are really scrumptious. They have an old-fashioned flavour.

⅓ cup shortening or margarine
¾ cup sugar
1 egg
¾ cup apple butter
½ cup milk
1 cup flour
1 tablespoon baking powder
½ teaspoon salt
½ teaspoon cinnamon
¾ cup rolled oats

Blend the shortening and sugar. Stir in the egg and apple butter, then the milk. Sift together the dry ingredients, and add oats. Pour the liquid apple-butter mixture over the flour mixture and stir just enough to moisten. Fill 12 buttered and floured muffin cups. Bake at 400°F for about 20 minutes. Spread apple butter over the top of each muffin and serve hot.

CHOCOLATE-CHIP MUFFINS

These are real company fare. You wouldn't dare make them when you are alone — not if you're watching your weight. Feather-light with chocolatey bits all through them and on top.

1 egg
1 cup milk
1 teaspoon vanilla
⅓ cup oil
1½ cups flour
½ cup sugar
1 tablespoon baking powder
¼ teaspoon salt
1 cup chocolate chips and a few more

Beat together the egg, milk, vanilla, and oil. Sift together the flour, sugar, and baking powder, and stir in chocolate chips. With as few strokes as possible stir the liquid into the dry ingredients. Bake at 375°F for 20 minutes. As soon as you take them from the oven, drop a few chocolate chips on top of each muffin. Remove to a rack and serve before they are cold. Mmmmmmmmmmmmmmmm . . . .

CHOCOLATE-CHIP CHOCOLATE MUFFINS

These should satisfy a chocoholic. Super, really chocolatey, high, light and impressive, especially if you ice them and dip them in chips as well.

1¾ cups flour
⅓ cup sugar
3 tablespoons cocoa
1 tablespoon baking powder
½ teaspoon salt
1 egg
¾ cup milk
½ cup oil
1 teaspoon vanilla
½ cup chocolate chips
Chocolate butter icing (optional)
Chocolate chips for topping (optional)

Sift together the dry ingredients. Blend egg, milk, oil, and vanilla. Pour over dry ingredients and stir until just blended as you add chocolate chips. Spoon batter into 12 buttered and floured muffin tins and bake at 400°F for 20 minutes. Remove from pan to a rack.

Slather with chocolate butter icing and sprinkle with chocolate chips or dip each muffin into icing and then into a dishful of chips. Fantastic! Extravagant!

COFFEE WALNUT MUFFINS

These are the quickest of all.

> **1 tablespoon instant coffee powder**
> **½ cup hot water**
> **½ cup whole milk or cream if you have it**
> **1 egg, beaten**
> **½ cup melted shortening, or vegetable oil if**
> **you're really in a rush**
> **2 cups flour**
> **1 teaspoon baking powder**
> **⅓ cup sugar**
> **1 teaspoon salt**
> **½ cup chopped walnuts**

Dissolve the coffee in the hot water, add the milk, egg, and shortening. Sift the flour, baking powder, sugar, and salt into a bowl. Stir in the walnuts. Pour the liquid ingredients into the dry and mix just enough to moisten them. Spoon the batter into 12 buttered muffin tins and bake in a 400°F oven for 20 minutes. The flavour is great.

DOUGHNUT MUFFINS

Both Norm and Eva gave me this recipe. Because they are irresistible I am giving you Eva's version — which is exactly twice as large as Norm's and makes 3 dozen.

> **3½ cups pastry flour, not sifted**
> **(Norm uses sifted all-purpose)**
> **1 tablespoon baking powder**
> **1 teaspoon salt**
> **½ teaspoon nutmeg**
> **1½ cups sugar**
> **2 eggs**
> **⅔ cup shortening or lard**
> **(Norm uses vegetable oil)**
> **1½ cups milk**
> **2 teaspoons vanilla**

Combine the flour, baking powder, salt, nutmeg, and sugar. In another bowl, beat the egg, shortening, milk, and vanilla. Add

to the dry ingredients and stir just enough to moisten. Fill
buttered muffin tins two-thirds full and bake at 350°F for 15 to
20 minutes. Tap the tins to dislodge the muffins. Eva says they
eat theirs dunked in maple syrup just like you would dough-
nuts. Norm's half-size recipe says: "Melt **1 cup butter** and roll
the hot muffins in it to coat them all over, then immediatley roll
them in a mixture of **2 cups sugar** and **2 teaspoons cinnamon**
to coat them like a doughnut. Eat them hot. They are scrumptious."

JAM AND OATMEAL MUFFINS

One day when half a dozen friends came for tea, I made three
kinds of muffins. They seemed to like these best.

1½ cups rolled oats
1½ cups buttermilk
1 egg
½ cup brown sugar
½ cup oil
1 teaspoon vanilla
1½ cups flour
1 tablespoon baking powder
½ teaspoon baking soda
½ teaspoon salt
¼ teaspoon nutmeg
4 tablespoons jam or marmalade

Stir oats and buttermilk together and let stand for at least 15
minutes, then add egg, sugar, oil, and vanilla. Sift together
flour, baking powder, baking soda, salt, and nutmeg. Add to
oats and stir until just mixed. Spoon into 12 buttered and
floured muffin cups. Spread 1 teaspoon of jam or marmalade on
top of each muffin. Bake at 400°F for 20 minutes. Remove to a
rack and serve warm.

RUM AND RAISIN MUFFINS

These won't make you stagger, they'll just make you feel good.

1 egg
½ cup sugar
½ cup oil
½ cup milk
¼ cup rum
½ cup raisins
2 cups flour
2 teaspoons baking powder
½ teaspoon baking soda
Pinch of salt
Sprinkle of nutmeg

Blend well the egg, sugar, oil, milk, and rum; add the raisins. (If you don't have or don't want to use real rum, you could use rum flavouring and ¼ cup more milk.) Sift the flour, baking powder, baking soda, and salt into the liquid mixture and stir until just moistened. Spoon into buttered muffin cups and sprinkle very lightly with nutmeg. Bake at 400°F for about 20 minutes and cool slightly on a rack before you indulge.

LIQUEUR MUFFINS

You could try this recipe with various liqueurs if you have them, or rye whisky. You might omit the raisins.

ZUCCHINI TARRAGON MUFFINS

These will mystify your guests. They are light and have a different flavour.

½ cup white sugar
½ cup brown sugar
½ cup oil
2 eggs
Grated rind of 1 orange
1 cup grated zucchini
1 cup flour or more
2 teaspoons baking powder
½ teaspoon baking soda
½ teaspoon salt
Pinch ground mace or ginger
2 teaspoons dried tarragon
½ cup chopped walnuts

Beat sugars, oil, eggs, orange rind, and zucchini. In another bowl, sift together the dry ingredients. Add tarragon and walnuts. Stir. Add zucchini mixture to flour mixture and stir until the flour is moistened — no more. Spoon into 18 well-buttered and floured muffin cups and bake at 350°F for 15 to 20 minutes. Remove to a rack and eat warm.

SAVOURY MUFFINS

*The number of savoury muffins you can make to serve with
a salad or soup or a meat course boggles the imagination.
You can really have fun with these.*

*Remember the Basic Muffin Recipe (page 3)? Use only 1
tablespoon of sugar instead of two, and add any number of
flavours to go with whatever you're serving.*

ONION MUFFINS

Finely mince **green or other onions** to make ⅓ cup and add it
to the Basic Muffin batter with the liquid ingredients.

PARSLEY MUFFINS

Snip **parsley** very fine until you have about ⅓ cupful; add it to
the liquid ingredients in the Basic Muffin batter. You could
combine parsley and onion if you like.

HERB MUFFINS

Add **1 tablespoon of fresh or dried herbs** to the Basic Muffin
batter. Try finely snipped dill. Sage is also wonderful — so are
basil, oregano, summer savoury, tarragon, or marjoram. Try
your favourite combination.

BACON OR HAM MUFFINS

Add **½ cup bacon bits** or crumbled fried bacon or finely cubed
ham to the basic batter. Use bacon dripping instead of shortening. Combine bacon with onions or herbs or parsley if you want
to be daring.

CHEESE MUFFINS

Parmesan Cheese sprinkled over muffins before or after they
come out of the oven gives a nice touch. So does grated Cheddar.

CORN AND CHEESE MUFFINS

Kit says these are substantial and go very well with a salad for lunch.

    2 cups flour
    ¼ cup sugar
    1 tablespoon baking powder
    1 teaspoon salt
    2 eggs
    1 can creamed corn
    ½ cup milk
    ½ cup grated Cheddar cheese
    ¼ cup oil or melted shortening

In a large bowl, combine the dry ingredients. Beat the eggs well. Stir in the corn, milk, cheese, and oil. Add corn mixture all at once to flour mixture. Stir just until moistened. Spoon batter into 12 buttered muffin cups and bake at 400°F for 25 minutes. Serve hot.

CHEDDAR BRAN MUFFINS

These are great to eat with a salad — or for breakfast with jam.

    1¼ cups buttermilk
    1 cup bran
    ¼ cup shortening
    ⅓ cup sugar
    1 egg
    1½ cups flour
    1½ teaspoons baking powder
    ½ teaspoon salt
    ¼ teaspoon baking soda
    1 cup shredded sharp Cheddar cheese

Pour buttermilk over bran and let stand till bran is softened. Cream the shortening and sugar. Beat in egg. Sift flour, baking powder, salt, and baking soda into the creamed mixture alternately with bran mixture. Stir in shredded cheese. Fill 12 buttered muffin cups, and bake at 400°F for about 20 minutes — or until golden. Serve immediately.

TOMATO MUFFINS

Great with an omelette or a salad. You can use canned tomato juice or V8 or simple puréed fresh tomatoes. Added Cheddar makes them better.

>   1 egg
>   ¼ cup oil
>   1 cup tomato juice
>   ½ cup finely grated Cheddar (optional)
>   1½ cups flour
>   2 teaspoons baking powder
>   ½ teaspoon baking soda
>   Pinch of salt

Blend the egg, oil, and tomato juice. Stir the Cheddar into the sifted dry ingredients and fold into the liquid ones until just moistened. Spoon into buttered muffin tins and bake at 400°F for about 20 minutes.

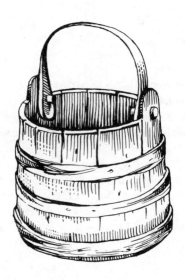

MUSHROOM MUFFINS

If you want muffins that are fantastic to eat with a salad or soup, try these.

1 egg
⅓ cup melted shortening or oil
¼ cup milk
1 can condensed cream of mushroom
  soup (undiluted)
2 cups pastry flour
3 teaspoons baking powder
¼ teaspoon salt
2 tablespoons cut-up parsley or chives (optional)

Beat the egg, blend in the shortening, milk, and soup. Sift together the flour, baking powder, and salt. Add the liquid mixture to the dry ingredients along with the parsley or chives, and stir only until the flour is moistened — remember the rule. Fill the buttered muffin tins two-thirds full and bake for 20 minutes at 425°F. You'll have 12 to 14 muffins that everyone will rave about.

I haven't yet had a chance to try them but I think these would be good with cream of tomato, chicken, celery, or asparagus soup as well, don't you?

QUICK BREADS

If you are the kind of person who likes always to have something on hand to offer to friends who knock at your door, you might be wise to develop a repertoire of quick breads. They can be mixed up as quickly as muffins, but take longer to bake. They need no rising as yeast breads do, need no icing as cakes do, and take up less space in your freezer. Sliced thin, lightly buttered — or not — or spread with cream cheese, they rest neatly on a saucer with a tea cup and are a pleasure to eat.

Their variety is infinite; you can put all sorts of things into them: dates, walnuts, sunflower seeds, honey, zucchini, raisins, bran, wheat germ, spices, oranges and lemons, bananas, cranberries, carrots, apples, currants, molasses, poppy seed, apricots, prunes, plums, pumpkin. You may think of more.

SALINA BAUMAN'S FRESH APPLE BREAD

Anything made with an apple is moist and good eating.

  1 cup sugar
  ½ cup margarine or butter
  2 eggs
  1½ tablespoons buttermilk or more
  1 cup peeled, chopped apples
  1 cup chopped nuts
  2 cups flour
  ½ teaspoon cinnamon
  ½ teaspoon baking soda
  ½ teaspoon salt

Cream sugar and margarine. Stir in eggs, buttermilk, chopped apples, and nuts. Sift in the flour, cinnamon, baking soda, and salt. Mix well, then turn into a well-buttered loaf pan. Bake at 350°F for about 45 minutes or until brown.

APPLE AND CHEESE NUT BREAD

Read the ingredients and see if you can resist trying this. I couldn't and I wasn't disappointed.

  ½ cup shortening
  ⅔ cup sugar
  2 eggs
  ¼ cup milk or more
  1 cup finely chopped apples, unpeeled
  ½ cup grated old Cheddar, or more
  ½ cup chopped walnuts
  2 cups flour
  1 teaspoon baking powder
  ½ teaspoon baking soda
  1 teaspoon salt

Cream the shortening; gradually add the sugar, and beat until fluffy. Add the eggs, one at a time, beating well after each one. Stir in the apples, milk, cheese, and nuts. Sift the flour, baking powder, baking soda, and salt into the other mixture and stir only until all the flour is dampened. Spoon into a buttered loaf pan, pushing the batter into the corners and sides of the pan. Bake at 350°F for about an hour. Serve sightly warm for the best effect.

APPLE AND CHEESE NUT MUFFINS

You could drop this batter into muffin tins, put them in a 400°F oven and have muffins in 20 minutes.

APPLESAUCE NUT BREAD

Got some applesauce in your fridge? Use it this way instead of slurping it up with cookies.

> 1¼ cups flour
> ¾ cup sugar
> 1 teaspoon salt
> 1 teaspoon baking powder
> ½ teaspoon baking soda
> ½ teaspoon cinnamon
> ¼ teaspoon nutmeg
> 1 cup rolled oats
> ½ cup chopped nuts
> 1¼ cups sweetened applesauce
> ¼ cup vegetable oil
> 2 eggs, beaten
> ¼ cup milk

Sift together the dry ingredients. Stir in the oats and nuts. Combine the applesauce, oil, eggs, and milk. Add to flour mixture, and stir just enough to moisten. Turn into a greased and floured loaf pan, and bake at 350°F for almost an hour. Remove from pan to a rack and try not to eat it until tomorrow, when it will slice more evenly.

APPLESAUCE NUT MUFFINS

Drop this batter into muffin tins and bake at 400°F for 20 minutes.

BANANA LOAF

There are times when there is a special on bananas at the local supermarket and I can't resist buying one of the fat yellow bundles. But bananas have a nasty habit of turning brown rather more quickly than I can eat them and I'm happily forced to make this lovely banana loaf.

2 cups flour
2 teaspoons baking powder
½ teaspoon baking soda
1 teaspoon salt
¼ cup shortening
½ cup sugar
2 eggs
2 ripe bananas (about 1 cupful, mashed)
1 teaspoon almond flavouring
½ cup buttermilk

Sift the flour, baking powder, baking soda, and salt. Cream the shortening and sugar, add eggs and mix well; add the mashed bananas and flavouring to the milk and add alternately with the flour mixture to the creamed mixture. When well blended, pour into a greased bread pan and bake at 350°F degrees for 45 minutes to an hour. Let cool and spread slices with butter.

THE BEST BANANA-NUT BREAD

Can anything be better than the best? Try this and prove it. It will stay moist for a week.

½ cup butter
1 cup sugar
3 bananas, mashed
2 eggs, beaten
¼ cup buttermilk
1 teaspoon baking soda
2 cups flour
½ cup chopped nuts

Cream the butter and sugar, then stir in the mashed bananas. Add eggs and mix well. Blend buttermilk and baking soda, then add to creamed mixture alternately with flour. Stir in the nuts and turn into a large buttered loaf pan or 2 small pans. Bake at 350°F for 1 hour. If you want to, you can add chopped maraschino cherries and chocolate chips.

CARROT BREAD

A visitor from France said this bread, on the fifth day of its life, had a subtle flavour — and ate several slices. (When Joyce Carter called to say she was bringing her friend to meet me, I had rejuvenated my little old loaf by dribbling over it a shot glass of Cointreau.)

> 1 cup sugar
> ½ cup oil
> 2 eggs, beaten
> 1 cup shredded carrots
> ½ cup milk
> 1½ cups flour
> 1 teaspoon baking powder
> 1 teaspoon baking soda
> ¼ teaspoon salt
> 1 teaspoon cinnamon
> ½ cup chopped walnuts
> ¼ cup Cointreau, rum, or brandy (entirely optional)

Mix the sugar and oil, add the eggs, stir in the carrot and milk. (If you have a blender put everything in it and give it a whirl till the carrots are chopped.) Sift the flour, baking powder, baking soda, salt, and cinnamon into the carrot mixture and stir just enough to blend, adding the walnuts as well. Bake in a buttered loaf pan for about 55 minutes in a 350°F oven.

You don't need the Cointreau if you eat this when it's fresh — actually you don't need it any time because the loaf stays moist. Do fashion editors make me show-off? The first time Joyce came to my cottage she wore white gloves, now she and her husband, Clay Derstine, come in their bare feet.

MARNIE'S CRANBERRY NUT BREAD

The red cranberries show up in each white slice — pretty as well as tasty. I won't guarantee it but you might try this recipe with a cupful of cranberry sauce if you don't have raw cranberries.

2 cups flour
1 cup sugar
1½ teaspoons baking powder
½ teaspoon baking soda
1 teaspoon salt
¼ cup shortening
1 egg, well beaten
¾ cup orange juice
Rind of 1 orange, chopped
½ cup chopped nuts
1 to 2 cups fresh cranberries, coarsely chopped

Sift the flour, sugar, baking powder, baking soda, and salt; cut in the shortening till the mixture is crumbly. Blend the egg with the orange juice and rind. (I put mine in my blender.) Pour all at once into the dry ingredients, mixing just enough to dampen. Gently fold in the nuts and the cranberries. Spoon the batter into a greased loaf pan, spreading the corners and sides slightly higher than the centre. Bake in a 350°F oven for about 1 hour, till the crust is golden and an inserted toothpick tells you it's baked through. Remove from the pan to cool on a rack.

CRANBERRY MUFFINS

If you'd rather have muffins, drop the batter into muffin tins and bake at 400°F for 20 minutes.

CHOCOLATE TEA BREAD

Lovely to have with afternoon tea or with a fruity dessert.

> ½ cup butter
> ⅔ cup sugar
> 1 egg
> 2 cups cake flour
> 1 teaspoon baking soda
> ¾ teaspoon salt
> ⅓ cup cocoa
> 1 teaspoon cinnamon
> 1 cup buttermilk
> 1 cup raisins
> ¾ cup chopped walnuts
> ¾ cup chocolate chips (optional)

Cream the butter. Add sugar gradually, creaming well. Add egg, beat well. Sift flour, baking soda, salt, cocoa, and cinnamon into the creamed mixture alternately with the buttermilk, beating until blended after each addition. Stir in raisins, walnuts, and chocolate chips. Turn into a buttered loaf pan. Bake at 350°F for about 1 hour. Cool on a rack.

KIT'S SUPER DELICIOUS CHOP SUEY QUICK BREAD

Kit brought me half a loaf of this and I couldn't resist eating all of it before the day was over.

> 2 cups flour
> 1 cup sugar
> 1 teaspoon baking powder
> ½ teaspoon baking soda
> ¼ teaspoon salt
> 2 tablespoons shortening
> 1 cup mixed peel
> ½ cup light raisins
> Candied ginger, as much as you please
> Juice of 1 orange and water to make 1 cup
> 1 egg, beaten
> 1 teaspoon vanilla

Sift together flour, sugar, baking powder, baking soda, and salt. Cut in shortening until well blended. Stir in peel, raisins, and ginger, coating well with flour. Combine orange juice and water, egg, and vanilla, and add all at once to dry ingredients. Blend thoroughly. Pour mixture into a greased loaf pan. Bake at 350°F for 50 to 60 minutes. Remove from pan to cool on a rack. It is so tasty that you don't have to butter the slices.

BEULAH'S PRESERVED GINGER LOAF

From Mother's old hand-written recipe book. Light as a feather and ready for love.

 ½ cup butter
 1 cup sugar
 3 eggs, beaten
 ½ cup milk
 ½ teaspoon salt
 2 cups flour
 1 teaspoon baking powder
 1 cup raisins
 ⅓ cup preserved ginger, chopped
 1 cup chopped nuts (¼ for topping)

Cream the butter and sugar, beat in the eggs, milk, and salt. Stir in the sifted flour and baking powder, just enough to moisten; blend in the raisins, preserved ginger, and ¾ cup nuts. Spoon into a greased loaf pan, sprinkle ¼ cup nuts over the batter and bake in a 250°F oven for over an hour.

GINGER MUFFINS

Simply drop the batter into greased muffin tins and bake at 400°F for 20 minutes. You should use fewer nuts.

GUMDROP BREAD

Children love things made with gumdrops — and so do adults.

> 3 cups flour
> ¾ cup sugar
> 1½ teaspoons baking powder
> 1 teaspoon salt
> ½ cup chopped nuts
> ½ cup raisins or chopped dates
> 1¼ cups cut-up gumdrops — but no black ones
> 1 egg, beaten
> 2 tablespoons melted butter, margarine, or oil
> 1½ cups milk

Sift the dry ingredients into a bowl and stir in the nuts, raisins, and gumdrops. Add the egg, butter, and milk, mixing only until the dry ingredients are moistened. Turn into a buttered loaf pan and bake at 350°F for an hour.

RUBY'S LEMON LOAF

Tender, moist, and finely textured. Everyone says, "This is the best lemon loaf I've ever tasted."

> ½ cup butter or margarine
> 1 cup sugar
> 2 eggs
> Grated rind of 2 lemons
> ½ cup milk
> 1½ cups flour
> 1 teaspoon baking powder
> ½ teaspoon salt
>
> *Topping:*
> ½ cup sugar
> Juice of 1 lemon

Cream the butter and sugar together, blend in the eggs and lemon rind then stir in the milk till the mixture is smooth. Sift the flour, baking powder, and salt into the mixture and stir just enough to moisten the dry ingredients. Pour into a buttered loaf pan and bake at 350°F for 45 to 55 minutes.

Meanwhile warm the ½ cup sugar in the lemon juice to dissolve the sugar. When the loaf comes from the oven, dribble the juice over the top and let it soak in. Leave the loaf in the pan for 10 minutes before you remove it to cool on a rack.

VARIATION: If you want to make this into an orange loaf, you need only substitute orange rind and juice. You might try a mixture of both.

ORANGE RAISIN OATMEAL BREAD

Liz Elstner is a pretty young lawyer who says she saves time, energy, and money by making two loaves at a time.

2 cups raisins
3¾ cups flour
2½ teaspoons salt
5 teaspoons baking powder
1¾ cups sugar
2½ cups rolled oats
¾ cup oil
2 eggs
Juice and grated rind of 2 large oranges
1¼ cups milk

Plump the raisins by pouring boiling water to cover them; let stand 10 minutes, then drain and pat dry with a paper towel. In a large bowl combine the flour, salt, baking powder, sugar, rolled oats, and raisins. Beat together the oil, eggs, orange juice, rind, and milk; pour over the dry ingredients, stirring only until they are moistened; you may need more orange juice or milk. Spoon the batter into 2 greased loaf pans, spreading evenly to all corners. Bake at 350°F for 50 to 60 minutes — or until done when tested with toothpick stuck in the centre. Cool on a rack for 10 minutes before removing from the pans. Eat one, freeze one.

ORANGE RAISIN OATMEAL MUFFINS

Drop the bread batter into muffin tins and bake at 400°F for 20 minutes. OR bake one dozen muffins and 1 loaf.

MOLASSES GRAHAM BREAD

Flavourful and moist and super served hot with butter melting into it — but it's good cold, too.

2 cups flour
1¾ cups graham or whole-wheat flour
¼ cup sugar
2 teaspoons salt
1½ teaspoons baking soda
1 teaspoon baking powder
⅓ cup shortening
2 eggs, beaten
1¾ cups buttermilk
¾ cup molasses

Sift dry ingredients and cut shortening into them. Blend eggs, buttermilk, and molasses; pour into dry mixture and stir just enough to blend all together. Pour into 2 greased loaf pans and bake in a 350°F oven for about 40 minutes. This keeps well and it can be frozen and reheated.

PINEAPPLE NUT BREAD

This one is easy to mix; easy to eat, too.

1 cup chopped nuts
Sugar for sprinkling
½ cup butter
¼ teaspoon grated lemon peel
¾ cup sugar
1 egg, beaten
2½ cups flour
2 teaspoons baking powder
1 teaspoon salt
½ teaspoon baking soda
¼ cup milk
1 can crushed pineapple

Put the nuts in a well-buttered loaf pan and shake to coat bottom and sides. Shake out excess nuts and reserve. Sprinkle pan with sugar. Blend butter and lemon peel until soft; add ¾ cup sugar. Beat in egg. Sift flour, baking powder, salt, and baking soda to gether into egg mixture alternately with milk and undrained pineapple; add reserved nuts, mix well. Spoon batter into loaf pan and let stand for 15 minutes before baking at 350°F for 50 minutes, or until toothpick inserted in centre comes out clean. Cool for 10 minutes then turn out on a rack.

PINEAPPLE NUT MUFFINS

Use ½ cup nuts in this batter then drop it into greased muffin tins and bake it at 400°F for 20 minutes.

NORM'S PINEAPPLE-ZUCCHINI BREAD

This makes two moist and delicious loaves — Norm's favourite. In the fall Norm grates her zucchini, wraps it in 2-cup packages and freezes it so she can make this throughout the winter.

> **3 eggs**
> **1 cup oil**
> **2 cups sugar**
> **2 teaspoons vanilla**
> **2 cups shredded zucchini (drained)**
> **1 can crushed pineapple (drained)**
> **3 cups flour**
> **2 teaspoons baking soda**
> **1 teaspoon salt**
> **¼ teaspoon baking powder**
> **1½ teaspoons cinnamon**
> **¾ teaspoon nutmeg**
> **1 cup raisins**
> **1 cup chopped nuts**

Beat the eggs, oil, sugar, and vanilla until thick. Stir in the zucchini and pineapple. Then sift together flour, baking soda, salt, baking powder, cinnamon, and nutmeg. Add raisins and nuts. Blend well with zucchini mixture. Pour into 2 buttered 9" x 5" loaf pans, and bake at 350°F for 1 hour. The loaf freezes well, too.

TANGY PLUM BREAD

You can make this quick bread with fresh or frozen plums. It is moist on the inside, crusty on the outside, and so flavourful that you'll be tempted beyond your capacity. I made this loaf to take to a friend, but cut off a piece to try it first, then another piece, then another — till I had to make another loaf to take to my friend.

> **2 cups flour**
> **½ cup sugar**
> **2½ teaspoons baking powder**
> **1 teaspoon salt**
> **½ cup chopped nuts**
> **1½ cups pitted and chopped plums**
> **1 egg, beaten**
> **¾ cup milk**
> **Grated rind of 1 orange**
> **3 tablespoons oil**

Sift together the flour, sugar, baking powder, and salt. Add the nuts and plums, and stir. In another bowl combine the egg, milk, orange rind, and oil. Blend, then pour the moist mixture into the flour-sugar mixture and blend only until there is no sign of flour. Spoon batter into a well-buttered loaf pan. Sprinkle the top with sugar and bake at 350°F for almost an hour, or until a toothpick inserted in the centre comes out clean. Cool on a rack — then try to resist it.

PRUNE BREAD

A good thing to make with those cooked prunes you forgot about. Almeda says, "You could even use schnitz and gwetcha (dried apples and prunes, cooked together)."

⅔ cup oil
1⅓ cups sugar
2 eggs, slightly beaten
⅔ cup buttermilk
⅔ to 1 cup chopped cooked prunes
1⅔ cups flour
½ teaspoon salt
½ teaspoon cinnamon
½ teaspoon cloves
½ teaspoon allspice (optional)
1⅓ teaspoons baking soda
½ cup chopped nuts

Beat together oil, sugar, and the eggs; stir in the buttermilk and whatever prunes you've found, but not much more than a cupful. Sift together into the liquid mixture the flour, salt, cinnamon, cloves, allspice, and baking soda; add the nuts. Pour the batter into a well-buttered loaf pan and bake at 350°F for half an hour, then reduce the heat to 325°F and bake another half hour. Let cool in the pan a few minutes before turning out on a rack. It will be moist, light, tasty, and will do you no end of good.

POPPY SEED LOAF

My friend Lorna gave me this recipe. She said, "Kids call it freckle bread and I've heard men jokingly refer to it as 'old people's L.S.D.' " I wonder why? It's moist and tasty but it didn't blow my mind.

> 1 cup sugar
> 2 eggs, slightly beaten
> 1 cup oil
> ½ cup evaporated milk
> 1½ cups flour
> 1½ teaspoons baking powder
> ½ teaspoon salt
> ½ cup poppy seeds (don't use stale ones;
>   they're bitter)
> Grated rind of 1 lemon

Beat the sugar with the eggs. Blend the oil and milk, then add them to the egg mixture alternately with the flour, baking powder, and salt, sifted together. Stir in the poppy seeds and lemon rind. Pour the batter into a well-buttered loaf pan. Sprinkle a few poppy seeds on top. Bake at 350°F for 45 minutes.

QUICK CHEESE BREAD

Lovely to eat with a salad or toasted in the morning with jam.

> 2 cups flour
> 2 teaspoons baking powder
> 1 teaspoon dry mustard
> 1 teaspoon salt
> Sprinkle of pepper
> 2 eggs, beaten
> ¼ cup melted butter or margarine
> ⅔ cup milk
> 1 cup grated Cheddar cheese

Sift dry ingredients together. Combine eggs, butter, and milk. Add to dry ingredients all at once and stir until flour is just moistened. Stir in cheese. Pour batter into a buttered loaf pan and bake at 375°F for almost an hour, or until a toothpick inserted in centre comes out clean. Cool for 10 minutes, then tip from the pan to a rack. Serve warm or cold.

TROPICAL LOAF

Lorna used to take this classy loaf to church bake sales when she lived near Carrying Place; it was always sold the minute she brought it in.

⅓ **cup buttermilk**
1 **cup bran**
1 **cup mashed bananas (3 medium)**
⅓ **cup shortening or oil**
⅔ **cup sugar**
2 **eggs**
1¼ **cups sifted flour**
½ **teaspoon salt**
1 **teaspoon baking powder**
½ **teaspoon baking soda**
¾ **cup chopped dried apricots**
½ **cup chopped filberts or pecans**
Honey for glaze

Pour the buttermilk over the bran. Add bananas and stir. Blend the shortening and sugar; add the eggs one at a time, beating well after each. Sift flour, salt, baking powder, and baking soda into the egg mixture alternately with the banana-buttermilk combination. Stir in the apricots and nuts. Pour into a buttered loaf pan, and bake at 350°F for 45 minutes. When it comes out of the oven, golden and gorgeous, brush the top with a glaze of warm honey.

Lorna says that sometimes, instead of 1 cup banana, she uses ¼ cup crushed pineapple and ¾ cup bananas. If the recipe is doubled you can make 3 small loaves or 2 regular-sized ones — and you don't have to take all of them to a bake sale.

LORNA'S BONANZA BREAD

Makes 2 loaves or 1 loaf and 18 muffins, supplies protein, calcium, iron, and vitamin A. Besides all that it has terrific flavour.

> 1 cup all-purpose flour
> 1 cup whole-wheat flour
> ⅔ cup dry milk powder
> ½ cup packed brown sugar
> ⅓ cup wheat germ
> 2 teaspoons baking powder
> ½ teaspoon baking soda
> ½ teaspoon salt
> ¼ cup chopped walnuts
> ½ cup chopped roasted peanuts
> ½ cup raisins
> 3 eggs
> ½ cup vegetable oil
> ½ cup molasses
> ¾ cup orange juice
> 1 cup mashed bananas (3)
> ⅓ cup chopped dried apricots or dried apple schnitz

Combine the dry ingredients, nuts, and raisins in a large bowl. Blend thoroughly. Whirl eggs in blender until foamy. Add oil, molasses, orange juice, and bananas, whirling after each addition. Add apricots; whirl to chop coarsely. Pour mixture into the bowl of dry ingredients. Stir only until moistened. Pour into 2 greased loaf pans. Bake at 325°F for 1 hour.

VARIATIONS: For a more tangy orange flavour, add ½ small orange, including peel to the blender ingredients. Use other nuts in place of walnuts if you like but don't substitute for peanuts which are used for nutritional balance. Instead of bananas you might substitute **raw chopped apple**, or **grated carrot, applesauce, peaches, pears, grated zucchini**.

Think of all the fun you can have trying all those; and good eating.

KIT'S CHEESE AND BEER LOAF

Light as a balloon, tender, and addictive — you won't be able
to stop eating this till it's all gone. Make it after a party and ease
your conscience by using the beer your friends have left in
bottles. The beer should be fairly flat and at room temperature.

2¾ cups flour
4 teaspoons baking powder
1 tablespoon sugar
½ teaspoon salt
½ teaspoon dry mustard
1 cup shredded sharp Cheddar cheese,
  the older the better
1 bottle (or 1½ cups) beer at room temperature

Topping:
¼ cup shredded Cheddar cheese
1½ tablespoons toasted sesame seeds

Sift together dry ingredients. Add cheese. Stir in beer just
enough to combine. Spoon batter into a buttered 8" x 4" loaf pan;
sprinkle top with cheese and seeds. Bake at 350°F for 45 to 50
minutes or until a toothpick stuck into the centre comes out
clean. Cool for a few minutes before turning out on a rack. Serve
warm with or without butter melting into it. To reheat, wrap
the loaf in foil and put it into a hot oven for 10 to 15 minutes. It
will be just as good as the first time.

CHRISTINA SCLANDERS' MIRACLE BEER BREAD

Ever run out of bread in your house? In exactly 1 hour and 5
minutes you can make a loaf with a crisp crust, a yeasty texture,
and great taste.

3 cups self-raising flour
3 tablespoons sugar
1 bottle of beer at room temperature

Mix the flour and sugar, pour the beer in — slowly, to prevent
frothing. Stir till the flour is moistened. Plop the dough into a

buttered loaf pan and bake it in a 350°F oven for 1 hour. Remove from pan and cool on a rack.

I could hardly wait to try this after Chris gave me her recipe. I had no self-raising flour, which is a homogenized combination of cake and pastry flour, baking powder, and salt; I improvised by adding 4 teaspoons of baking powder and a teaspoon of salt to all-purpose flour. The result was not as good as the bread I'd eaten at Chris' house — but not bad. I'm going to keep on experimenting. I've also bought a package of self-raising at the supermarket — to be prepared for emergencies.

PUMPKIN NUT BREAD

A good way to use up that extra cup of pumpkin you have cooked and mashed. The bread freezes well for future reference.

> ¼ cup softened butter or margarine
> 1 cup sugar
> 2 eggs
> 1 cup cooked and mashed pumpkin
> ½ cup milk
> 2 cups flour
> 2 teaspoons baking powder
> ½ teaspoon baking soda
> 1 teaspoon salt
> 1 teaspoon cinnamon
> ½ teaspoon nutmeg
> 1 cup chopped nuts
> ½ cup raisins (optional)

Cream butter and sugar. Beat in the eggs, then the pumpkin and milk. Stir in the dry ingredients sifted together until blended. Stir in nuts and raisins, and turn into a well-buttered and floured loaf pan. Bake at 350° for 45 to 55 minutes, or until toothpick inserted in centre comes out clean. Cool on a rack, slice, butter, and enjoy.

PUMPKIN MUFFINS

Use ½ cup nuts in batter and drop it into greased muffin tins; bake at 400°F for 20 minutes.

Date and Raisin Breads

One stormy February night when I spoke to the Kitchener-Waterloo Newcomer's Club, the ladies clustered around me to chat and have books autographed. One of them was a neat, precise lady who told me she had been brought up in the Appenzell region of northern Switzerland where the dialect of the mountain people had not changed in more than 600 years. She said she longed to meet my Old Order Mennonite friends, whose forebears had come from Switzerland 300 years ago to see if their dialect in any way resembled her own.

It was September before we were able to arrange the meeting. While we sat round Hannah's kitchen table and drank tea, ate Chelsea buns, squares that Eva had brought, and Hannah's pull buns, Alice Raab, the Swiss lady, told us about her country and talked in her dialect. I understood only one word — Huntly, meaning dog. Hannah and Eva understood much more, but they said they thought their own Pennsylvania Dutch dialect had over the years become more or less "Englishified."

At the end of the week of our meeting, Alice went to Switzerland for a visit and, after her return to her home in Waterloo, brought me a bottle of Alpenzeller Alpenbitter, an aperitif made from the flowers of herbs that grow in the Appenzell Mountains and is not exported. Whenever I have gone to Switzerland I have brought home a bottle. It has a sort of wild licorice-root flavour and speaks with authority.

Next time Alice came to my house, she brought me a loaf she had made. She said it is a great favourite in Appenzell and is especially delicious served with red wine. It stays moist and keeps well — unless you can't resist it.

ROSINEN-SCHNITTEN

Alice says, "This is a very old recipe. It was handed down from generation to generation of my father's family. It is simple, inexpensive, and very popular served with a bottle of red wine as a treat for unexpected visitors."

2 cups sugar
3 eggs
1 teaspoon cinnamon
¼ teaspoon ground cloves
Pinch of salt
2 cups flour
2 cups currants
1 or 2 tablespoons Kirsch

Mix sugar, eggs, cinnamon, cloves, and salt together until foamy. Add remaining ingredients. Put the mixture into a loaf pan lined with greased paper, and bake at 350°F for 1 hour and 15 minutes. Cool on a rack. When cold, cut in slices, then cut each slice into two pieces. Store slices in a cookie tin. They will keep a long time.

GRAHAM FRUIT BREAD

Light, smooth, and easy to mix. Recipe makes 2 loaves.

1 cup flour
2 teaspoons baking powder
½ cup sugar
1 teaspoon salt
2 cups graham flour
½ cup raisins or chopped dates
½ cup chopped walnuts
1 cup buttermilk
1 cup milk
1 teaspoon baking soda
½ cup molasses

Sift the flour with baking powder, sugar, and salt; add and stir in the graham flour, raisins, and nuts. Add buttermilk and milk and stir until the mixture is just blended. Beat the baking soda into the molasses with a fork until it is foamy, then quickly add to the other mixture and stir until blended — no more. Turn into 2 greased loaf pans and bake in a 350°F oven for 45 minutes.

SHERRY DATE LOAF

Doris Lewis made this loaf for a morning meeting of the Ayr Public Library Book Club where I was speaking. It was wonderful, the best loaf I've ever eaten. Doris said, "I used medium-dry sherry of good quality, butter, and pecans, but I think walnuts would be as good. I am going to add some chopped preserved ginger next time."

    1 cup sherry
    2 cups chopped dates
    2 cups flour
    1 teaspoon baking powder
    1 teaspoon baking soda
    ¼ teaspoon salt
    ¼ cup shortening or butter
    1 cup brown sugar
    1 egg
    ¼ cup chopped candied cherries
    ½ cup chopped nuts

Bring sherry to boiling point and pour over the dates. Let cool, stirring 2 or 3 times. Sift dry ingredients. Cream shortening and sugar; add egg and beat until fluffy. Add the dry ingredients alternately with the date-sherry mixture. Blend in the cherries and nuts. Put in a loaf pan lined with buttered waxed paper. Bake at 350°F for 50 to 60 minutes. Allow to mellow at least one day before cutting.

RUM AND DATE LOAF

Norm sometimes serves this to her several bridge clubs; they love it. It's rich and rummy and moist.

>1½ cups dates
>1 cup walnuts
>1 teaspoon baking soda
>1 cup boiling water
>½ cup butter
>1 cup brown sugar
>2 eggs, beaten
>1 cup flour
>½ teaspoon salt
>1 teaspoon vanilla
>4 tablespoons rum
>1 teaspoon water

Chop the dates and nuts. Add the baking soda to boiling water and pour over dates and nuts; let stand while preparing batter. Cream butter and gradually add the sugar; add eggs. Pour date mixture into this and mix well. Sift flour and salt into the mixture and stir just enough to moisten; add vanilla last.

Pour into buttered loaf pan and bake at 350°F for about an hour. Remove from oven and pour over it the rum mixed with a little water. Allow to cool on a rack and try to resist temptation.

BEVVY'S BRAN BREAD

"Wonderful easy" to make, moist and delicious.

>1 cup brown sugar
>2 cups bran
>2 cups flour
>2 teaspoons baking soda
>1 teaspoon salt
>2 cups buttermilk
>1 cup raisins
>½ cup coarsely chopped nuts

Mix sugar and bran with sifted flour, baking soda, and salt. Add buttermilk and stir in raisins and nuts. Pour into a loaf pan and bake in a 350°F oven for almost an hour.

JEAN SALTER'S BRAN LOAF

Turn to Jean Salter's Bran Muffins (page 30); sometimes she puts the batter into a well-buttered loaf pan instead of muffin tins. She bakes it in a 350°F oven for about 40 minutes. Butter it while it is still warm and there won't be any left when it's cold.

GRANOLA OR GRAPENUTS RAISIN BREAD

Ruby says this loaf is full of surprises — depending on what you've put in your granola.

1¾ cups all-purpose flour
1 cup brown or white sugar
4 teaspoons baking powder
1½ teaspoons salt
1½ teaspoons cinnamon
1 cup whole-wheat flour
1½ cups granola (or grapenuts)
1½ cups raisins
2 eggs, well beaten
1⅓ cups milk
⅓ cup melted butter or margarine
1 teaspoon vanilla

Sift the white flour, sugar, baking powder, salt, and cinnamon together. Stir in the whole-wheat flour, granola, and raisins. Combine the eggs, milk, butter, and vanilla; pour all at once into the dry ingredients, stirring just until moistened. Turn into a greased 9" x 5" loaf pan — or 2 smaller ones — sprinkle granola or grapenuts on top and pat down lightly. Bake in a 350°F oven for 50 to 60 minutes, testing with a toothpick stuck in the middle. Cool on a rack for 10 minutes before removing from the pan. Slice and butter it to serve with a nice cup of tea — or have it with fruit or cheese for dessert.

MOTHER'S DATE BREAD

A good keeper.

Beat together till creamy:

> ½ cup sugar
> Butter the size of an egg
> ½ teaspoon salt

Combine and add to first mixture:

> 1½ cups cut-up dates
> 1 cup chopped walnuts
> 1 cup boiling water
> 1 teaspoon soda

Then add:

> 1½ cups flour
> 1 teaspoon baking powder

Pour into a loaf pan and bake at 375°F till it tests done — about 45 minutes. Slice, butter, and serve.

SALEMA HOLLINGER'S MOLASSES WHOLE-WHEAT BREAD

A light quick bread, tender and moist, with no shortening, and that old-fashioned flavour.

> 1 teaspoon salt
> 1 teaspoon baking soda
> ¾ cups all-purpose flour
> 2 cups whole-wheat or graham flour
> 1 egg, beaten
> ½ cup molasses
> ½ cup brown sugar
> 1½ cups buttermilk
> 1 cup chopped dates or raisins

Mix the salt, baking soda, and two kinds of flour together. Beat the egg with the molasses and brown sugar, then add the buttermilk. Pour the liquid ingredients into the dry, add the dates, and stir only until moistened. Pour into a buttered loaf pan, bake in a 350°F oven for about 40 minutes, till the bread tests done. Butter it and serve it still warm if you want to hear your guests purr with great satisfaction.

HONEY RAISIN NUT LOAF

When Mrs. Orval Honsberger brought this to a Lutheran church bake sale, it was snapped up immediately. Somebody knew a good thing.

¾ cup boiling water
1½ cups raisins
½ cup chopped walnuts
¼ cup butter
⅓ cup brown sugar
1 egg
½ cup honey
1 teaspoon rum extract, or 1 tablespoon rum
1¾ cups flour
½ teaspoon salt
1 teaspoon baking soda
⅓ cup milk

Add boiling water to the raisins and nuts; let stand until cool. Cream the butter, sugar, egg, honey, and rum until light and fluffy. Sift the flour, salt, and baking soda into the creamed mixture alternately with the cooled, drained raisins and the milk, stirring only until smooth. Pour into a buttered loaf pan and bake at 350°F for 50 to 60 minutes. All quick breads taste better if you eat them soon after they come out of the oven.

DATE LOAF WITH RAISINS

Marnie Paisley inherited this old favourite from Miss Emma Kaufman, who was known by many people in the world of the YWCA in Canada and Japan.

1 teaspoon baking soda
1 cup dates, cut in pieces
1 cup raisins
Grated rind of 1 orange
1 cup boiling water
1 cup white or brown sugar
4 tablespoons butter
1 egg
1¼ cups flour
½ teaspoon salt
½ cup broken walnuts

Sprinkle the baking soda over the dates, raisins, and orange rind, and pour the boiling water over them. Let cool. Cream sugar and butter, beat in the egg and stir into the date-raisin mixture when it has cooled. Sift the flour and salt into the bowl with the rest and stir only until it is blended. Fold in the nuts. Pour into a loaf tin, well buttered, and bake at 350°F for about 55 minutes. This keeps well for some time; it freezes well, too.

ABERDOVEY FRUIT BREAD

At a bed-and-breakfast home facing the sea in Wales a generous hostess gave us this delicious bread with a cup of tea before we retired.

½ **cup shortening**
¼ **cup sugar**
¼ **cup molasses**
1 **egg**
3 **cups flour**
1½ **teaspoons salt**
¼ **teaspoon baking soda**
1½ **cups buttermilk**
1½ **cups raisins, chopped**
1¼ **cups currants, chopped**
¼ **cup chopped citron or chopped lemon rind**

Cream shortening and sugar. Beat in the molasses and then the egg. Alternately add the dry ingredients sifted together and the buttermilk. Stir in the fruit. Spoon the batter into two greased loaf pans and bake at 325°F for 1 to 1¼ hours. These loaves will stay moist if you give them a chance. You can freeze one if you don't trust yourself.

Special Breads

MOTHER'S JOHNNY CAKE

In the spring when the sap is running, I yearn for Mother's Johnny Cake; it was a supper treat, served hot from the oven and drenched with fresh maple syrup. (Of course we were just skinny little girls in those days.)

1 cup flour
1 cup cornmeal
1 cup sugar
1 teaspoon baking soda
2 tablespoons butter
1 egg
1 cup sour cream
Cinnamon for sprinkling

Blend flour, cornmeal, sugar, baking soda, and butter. Beat the egg into the sour cream, then stir into the flour mixture. Smooth the stiff batter into a 9" x 9" cake pan. Sometimes I sprinkle the top with cinnamon before I bake it. Bake at 350°F for 35 minutes. It is great for breakfast too — or after a salad lunch or supper. Norm served it to her bridge club and the whole cake was demolished. Everyone had a second helping.

MRS. ABNER EBY'S ORANGE GINGERBREAD

This is the best gingerbread I've ever tasted; it has terrific flavour, texture, tenderness, and style. With a glaze on top.

1 cup orange juice
(fresh, frozen, or dissolved crystals)
Rind of 1 orange
1 cup butter or margarine
1 cup molasses
1 cup brown sugar
3 eggs, beaten
2½ cups flour
1 teaspoon salt
1½ teaspoons baking soda
1 teaspoon cinnamon
1 teaspoon allspice
2 teaspoons ginger

Glaze:
1½ cups icing sugar
Enough orange juice to make it pour

In your blender put the orange juice and rind; blend till the rind is ground up. In a saucepan melt the butter, add the brown sugar and molasses, pour in the orange juice mixture and heat until the sugar is dissolved — don't let it boil. Cool, then beat in the eggs. Sift the dry ingredients over the wet ones and stir only until blended. Pour into a large cake pan, about 9" x 13", and bake at 325°F for about an hour. While it is baking make a glaze of icing sugar and enough orange juice to make it pour easily, but not too thin. When the gingerbread comes out of the oven, pour the glaze over it while it is hot and spread it evenly. Let the gingerbread cool on a rack in the pan. Serve it with whipped cream or ice cream as a dessert or with a cup of tea any time. It's a big cake but it won't last long.

MOIST AND TENDER GINGERBREAD

I baked this one day when two people came for tea; we ate quite a bit and I finished the rest over the next three days. Slightly warmed in my little toaster oven, it was just as good as at the beginning.

½ cup brown sugar
½ cup shortening
1 egg, slightly beaten
½ cup molasses
½ cup boiling water
1⅓ cups flour
1teaspoon cinnamon
1 teaspoon ginger
½ teaspoon allspice
½ teaspoon salt
½ teaspoon baking powder
½ teaspoon baking soda

Beat together the first 5 ingredients. Sift the rest together, add to liquid mixture and blend well. Pour the batter into 8- or 9-inch square pan and bake at 350°F for 30 to 40 minutes. Serve slightly warm with whipped cream, whipped cottage cheese, or apple sauce.

IRISH SODA BREAD

At Rundles Restaurant in Stratford they sometimes serve fresh soda bread with the first course. Often they shape it into neat, round buns.

1 cup all-purpose flour
1 cup whole-wheat flour
1 teaspoon baking soda
1 teaspoon salt
⅛ cup margarine
1 cup buttermilk

Sift the flours into a bowl with baking soda and salt. Rub in the margarine; make a well in the centre and add the buttermilk.

Knead until smooth and free from stickiness. Form into loaves, make a cut across each — a cross for good luck. Bake at 325°F for about 40 minutes.

SUSAN MACMAHON'S CURRANT SODA BREAD

This was handed down by my Irish great-grandmother. There's no wonder that it survived. Try it with Irish coffee.

4 cups flour
¼ cup sugar
3 teaspoons baking powder
1 teaspoon baking soda
1 teaspoon salt
¼ teaspoon nutmeg
2 cups currants
¼ cup butter or margarine
1 egg, slightly beaten
1¾ cups buttermilk

Combine all the dry ingredients. Add the butter and work in until crumbly. (I let my electric mixer do it — wouldn't Susan have loved that?) Stir in the currants. Mix the egg with the buttermilk, add to the dry mixture and stir until blended. Turn out on a floured board and knead for a couple of minutes till smooth. Divide the dough in half and form each part into a round loaf; press each loaf into a greased pie plate. With a sharp knife cut about an inch deep into the tops of the loaves as if your were slicing a pie. Sprinkle sugar on the loaves. Bake in a 375°F oven for about 40 minutes. Butter and eat hot. It stays moist for several days.

MUSTARD HOT BREAD

"Maybe somebody started making gingerbread and put in mustard by mistake," Bevvy told me. Anyway, it's a winner.

½ cup shortening
½ cup sugar
1 egg, well beaten
2½ cups flour
1 teaspoon cinnamon
½ teaspoon ground cloves
1 teaspoon dry mustard
1½ teaspoons baking soda
1 teaspoon salt
1 cup hot water
1 cup molasses

Cream the shortening and sugar till smooth. Add the egg and beat till well blended. Sift the flour, spices, mustard, baking soda, and salt. Combine the hot water and molasses and add to the creamed mixture alternately with the flour mixture. Pour into a well-greased 9" x 9" cake pan and bake in a 350°F oven for about 35 minutes. Serve while it is still warm in thick buttered slices. Your guests will protest about putting on pounds but they'll all take three or four pieces.

INDEX